MEL BAY PRESENT

BY STAN WHITMIRE
TRANSCRIBED BY LINDA CUMMINGS

1 2 3 4 5 6 7 8 9 0

Visit us on the Web at www.melbay.com — E-mail us at email@melbay.com

Contents

Blessed Assurance

Fanny J. Crosby, Phoebe P. Knapp
Arr. Stan Whitmire
Transcr. Linda M. Cummings

8

*This page has been
left blank to avoid
awkward page turns*

Sweet Hour of Prayer/
I Must Tell Jesus

Arr. Stan Whitmire

Transcr. Linda M. Cummings

I Must Tell Jesus

Swing eighths

The Love of God
Medley

Arr. Stan Whitmire

Transcr. Linda M. Cummings

16

This page has been
left blank to avoid
awkward page turns

Great is Thy Faithfulness

Thomas O. Chisholm, William M. Runyon
Arr. Stan Whitmire
Transcr. Linda M. Cummings

The Grace of God
Medley

Arr. Stan Whitmire
Transcr. Linda M. Cummings

He Giveth More Grace

29

Grace, Grace (Greater Than Our Sin)

Jesus Paid It All

Elvina M. Hall, John T. Grape

Arr. Stan Whitmire

Transcr. Linda M. Cummings

*This page has been
left blank to avoid
awkward page turns*

God Leads Us Along/
He Hideth My Soul

G. A. Young

Fanny Crosby, William J. Kirkpatrick

Arr. Stan Whitmire

Transcr. Linda M. Cummings

He Hideth My Soul

41

It Is Well

Horatio G. Spafford, Philip P. Bliss

Arr. Stan Whitmire

Transcr. Linda M. Cummings

48

Jesus Is All the World to Me/
What a Friend We Have in Jesus

Will L. Thompson

Joseph M. Scriven, Charles C. Converse

Arr. Stan Whitmire

Transcr. Linda M. Cummings

I Need Thee Every Hour/I Surrender All/
'Tis So Sweet to Trust in Jesus

Annie S. J. Hawks, Rev. Robert Lowry/
Judson W. Van de Venter, Winfield S. Weeden/
Louisa M. R. Stead, William J. Kirkpatrick

Arr. Stan Whitmire

Transcr. Linda M. Cummings

With reflection ♩ = 72

I Need Thee Every Hour

Tempo I

'Tis So Sweet to Trust in Jesus

Wonderful Peace

W. D. Cornell, W. G. Cooper

Arr. Stan Whitmire

Transcr. Linda M. Cummings